D0588076

Wholehearted

60 days for

CWR

Contents

Give it all!

When someone asked Jesus what the most important thing for us to do in life is, He replied: 'Love the Lord your God with all your heart and with all your soul and with all your mind' (Matt. 22:37). We were created to love God with our *everything* and we are called to have a faith that is wholehearted.

We looked up 'wholehearted' in a thesaurus and have come up with a definition of wholehearted faith:

To be impassioned with a genuine, unquestioning and never-failing faith, which stands, unwavering, in the face of our fears, doubts and weaknesses and says: 'I trust in God and I'm going to put my whole life in His hands.'

That's quite a challenge, isn't it? But it is possible! Yes, we are called to be wholehearted for God, but did you know, He is already, and always has been – from the beginning of time – wholehearted in His love for you! His love is unfaltering, unreserved, determined, enduring … wow! So let's give God our whole love and life in return.

In this book we're going to dive into the following: **Plans of the Heart** is about the decisions we make and paths we take, and how we choose wisely. **Who's First?** looks at what and who we put first in our everyday lives and how we can get God at the centre of everything. Then, **Heart Clear Out** uncovers the things we might be harboring in our hearts, like jealousy or deceitfulness, and explores how we get rid of these things that hold us back. Next up, **Unshaken** explores some biblical examples of people up against challenges and pressure, and what we can learn from their steadfast faith. Finally, we look at the **Heart of Jesus**, a heart that is completely for us – the perfect example of wholeheartedness!

Enjoy!

Plans of the Heart

'To humans belong the plans of the heart, but from the LORD comes the proper answer of the tongue … Commit to the LORD whatever you do, and he will establish your plans. The LORD works out everything to its proper end – even the wicked for a day of disaster … In their hearts humans plan their course, but the LORD establishes their steps.'

PROVERBS 16:1,3–4,9

We make plans in our head (I'm going to go shopping at twelve o'clock) but we also make much more important plans in our hearts (I'm going to follow Jesus; I'm going to be a doctor one day). **God knows all the plans we make, big and small,** and He wants to reveal to us *the* plan for our whole lives: His plan.

One way to get our plans aligned with His is to read the Bible. A particularly good book in helping us with planning and choosing wisely is Proverbs.

King Solomon (the guy who wrote most of the wise words in Proverbs) was invited by God to ask Him for anything he wanted. And what did he ask for? A huge palace filled to the rooftops with diamonds? No! He asked God to make him a *wise* leader. And God did just that (1 Kings 3:4–14; 4:29–34).

What was so special about Solomon's wisdom? And how is his advice going to be better than that given by our magazine agony aunts? The answer is found in verse seven. Solomon's wisdom originates from God. It isn't an 'I think ...' wisdom but a 'God says ...' wisdom. It begins with an acceptance that God knows best – because God knows everything!

Just remember, God put those plans in your heart and He is going to help you live them out in the right way. So you can wholeheartedly give your plans to Him!

Engage **Do you really believe God knows best? Ask God to wise you up to His ways of thinking and behaving, so you can really know Him more.**

Begin the search

'if you call out for insight and cry aloud for understanding, and if you look for it as for silver and search for it as for hidden treasure, then you will understand the fear of the LORD and find the knowledge of God. For the LORD gives wisdom; from his mouth come knowledge and understanding. He holds success in store for the upright, he is a shield to those whose way of life is blameless, for he guards the course of the just and protects the way of his faithful ones. Then you will understand what is right and just and fair – every good path. For wisdom will enter your heart, and knowledge will be pleasant to your soul. Discretion will protect you, and understanding will guard you.' **PROVERBS 2:3–11**

Solomon lists some of the things we need to do to tap into God's wisdom.

1. Listen in. God speaks through His Word (the Bible), so use it! Also listen to others teaching from the Bible. **Find out all you can about God.**

2. Think about it. Don't let wisdom from God go in one ear and out the other. It's too important for your life to let it slip like that. Think how it applies to you. Memorise it.

3. Pray about it. If you need help understanding bits then go to the Writer Himself. Ask Him to show you the best thing to do in every situation.

4. Search for the right way. Many of life's problems don't have easy answers. Wisdom is as rare as a shooting star. You don't always discover the right thing to do straight away. That's why it's vital to pray and soak up the Bible regularly, and even ask the advice of experienced Christians.

5. Believe God has the answer. Solomon found that God knows the best way to deal with any situation and looks after those facing difficult problems.

Engage

The original wise men travelled for nearly two years following a star to track down Jesus. The kingdom of God is like treasure hidden in a field (Matt. 13:44). So we need to search, dig deep and persevere in our faith today.

Pray

Lord Jesus, as I search for You and Your wisdom, may I find You. Amen.

Learn from their mistakes

'A fool spurns a parent's discipline, but whoever heeds correction shows prudence … Mockers resent correction, so they avoid the wise … A wise son brings joy to his father, but a foolish man despises his mother … Plans fail for lack of counsel, but with many advisors they succeed.' **PROVERBS 15:5,12,20,22**

So you're planning to go to a party. All your friends are going, it's a done deal – you've got to go. But wait, it's a Halloween party; you know your parents said no last year. But it's worth a shot this year, right? … Cue the barrage of: 'This is so unfair', 'You're so boring' and 'Why can't I?'

So they said no. What do you do now? Solomon's advice is to listen to your parents. If you don't get their reasoning for what you should or shouldn't do, then talk things through with them. And respect their decision.

You've probably heard the line said by many young people, 'I have to learn from my own mistakes'. The truth is, yes we do all make mistakes and they do help us grow wiser, but are there instances where we should just trust our parents?

Let's put it this way, if a mum saw her beautiful baby girl crawl over to an open fire, would she sit back and think,

'Oh it's OK, she just needs to learn from this herself'? No way! She'd be over there like a shot, *preventing* the mistake, because *she knows the consequence.*

And that's just it. Your parents are more likely to know the consequences and they don't want you to suffer them.

It's wise to ask your parents' advice because **your plans are more likely to succeed with their support,** knowledge and experience. It can be really hard to take the next wise step, which is to obey them, but do it!

 It's also true that parents or guardians may not always be right, particularly when you want to follow Jesus but they aren't Christians. Nonetheless, God chose our parents for us and He promises us something amazing if we respect them: 'Honour your father and your mother, as the LORD your God has commanded you, so that you may live long and that it may go well with you in the land the LORD your God is giving you' (Deut. 5:16).

Influence

'if sinful men entice you, do not give in to them. If they say, "Come along with us …" my son, do not go along with them, do not set foot on their paths; for their feet rush into evil, they are swift to shed blood. How useless to spread a net where every bird can see it! These men lie in wait for their own blood; they ambush only themselves! Such are the paths of all who go after ill-gotten gain; it takes away the life of those who get it.'

PROVERBS 1:10–11,15–19

It's easy to get sucked into the crowd. Not wanting to be the odd one out, many people have been pressurised into doing things they don't want to do. We become part of the tug of war between following God and following our friends.

So what does today's reading mean for us? Does it say that we should put ourselves into a snuggly Christian bubble, shutting ourselves off from the world? Well, we know that it's really important to be friends with those who aren't Christians, because how else are they going to hear about God? Perhaps what this particular reading is warning us against is influence. **Who is influencing who?**

If your friends respect your faith and the way you live, then you are more able to be a positive influence in their lives. But if you know that they don't, and perhaps you're the only Christian in the group, you can be sure to come up against peer pressure that will be a negative influence.

And it can happen slowly and in a very subtle way. The little compromises we make to be part of the action gradually soften our defences and leave us open to bigger temptations and pitfalls.

So if you know your crowd is leading you into trouble, think whether it's worth it: are you influencing them for good or are you being influenced?

 Engage

Buffalo are some of the biggest and toughest animals in the world, but they have two weaknesses. If one runs, they all stampede. They are also short-sighted. The North American Indians hunted them by causing one to run towards a cliff edge or pit. The rest would follow and stampede to their deaths. Don't be stampeded into areas God wants to protect you from. Follow Him and you will be safe.

Decisions, decisions

'Let love and faithfulness never leave you; bind them round your neck, write them on the tablet of your heart. Then you will win favour and a good name in the sight of God and man. Trust in the LORD with all your heart and lean not on your own understanding; in all your ways submit to him, and he will make your paths straight.' **PROVERBS 3:3–6**

Making important decisions isn't easy. We battle over the pros and cons, think about how our life would be affected, wonder if we're making a mistake … It can be a real headache!

During the next few years you'll make some key decisions about what you want to do with the rest of your life. Scary stuff! But don't fear, God is with us and He gives us some great advice.

The hot tip is: don't rush into making decisions without chatting things through with God first. The temptation is to think we know best, but God, who made us and everything in creation, really knows best because He knows the best possible future for us. He wants us to reach our full potential so **we should trust every stepping stone he lays down.**

If things don't always work out as we hoped, if our plans fail, we should keep trusting that God has our best interests at heart and there will be other opportunities around the corner. He sometimes needs to straighten us out before He can 'make our paths straight'.

 **Engage**

A pilot was trying to land his small aircraft in poor visibility and, knowing there was a tall building in his flight path, called the control tower for help. The reply was reassuring: 'Just follow my instructions and I'll deal with the obstructions.' God offers us the same reassurance for our lives. Trust Him with every decision.

Pray

Lord, I thank You that You know best and want the best for my life. I commit to following Your instructions; keeping to the right path. Amen.

trust

Check your motive

'All a person's ways seem pure to them, but motives are weighed by the LORD … The LORD detests all the proud of heart. Be sure of this: they will not go unpunished. Through love and faithfulness sin is atoned for; through the fear of the LORD evil is avoided. When the LORD takes pleasure in anyone's way, he causes their enemies to make peace with them. Better a little with righteousness than much gain with injustice.'

PROVERBS 16:2,5–8

Behind every decision we make, whether we're aware of it or not, is a motive. A motive is what makes us decide to do something, eg, we buy those shoes because we want to look good; we help our friend because we want to keep that friendship; we eat because we're hungry! These motives can be hard to uncover because they come from our hearts.

As today's Bible reading advises, sometimes our motives can be wrong or simply selfish, and we need God to help us see this and sort them out. A decision may seem perfectly OK to us, even the right thing to do, but if we dig a little deeper, **we might find that our motives are wrong.**

Solomon's father, David, had decided to build a temple in Jerusalem. What could be wrong with that? He and his advisor, the prophet Nathan, started getting excited about the project, but neither bothered to consult God. Although it was the right decision, it was the wrong time. God wanted a temple, but He wanted it built in Solomon's reign, not David's. David wisely fell in line with God's wishes and when the Temple was eventually built, God filled it with His glory.

God helps us make wise decisions on the basis of what He wants to do – not what we want to do. However, this always works in our favour because when we get involved in God's plans we have His 100 per cent support and backing.

Think about a decision you've made recently and ask yourself, honestly, was it made in order to please God or people or yourself? The only motives that bring true success are those that want to please God.

On the right path

'The path of the righteous is like the morning sun, shining ever brighter till the full light of day. But the way of the wicked is like deep darkness; they do not know what makes them stumble … Let your eyes look straight ahead; fix your gaze directly before you. Give careful thought to the paths for your feet and be steadfast in all your ways. Do not turn to the right or the left; keep your foot from evil.' **PROVERBS 4:18–19,25–27**

The word 'righteous' can be understood as meaning 'to be right with God'. So the righteous path is the right path. God has planned every step for us. **We don't need to stumble through life.** We can know exactly where we're heading, and that is eternity with God!

It's important to know that the devil doesn't want you to make it. He will throw all he can at you to tempt you to look to 'the right or the left', because when you do, your eyes lose sight of God and so lose sight of what is right or wrong. That's why we need to 'look straight ahead' to Jesus.

Here are some practical ways to keep your feet set on the path and your eyes fixed on God:

- Pay attention to God's commands and don't push Him to the back of your mind when making decisions (Prov. 4:20).
- Guard your heart. If your conscience flashes a warning light, don't switch it off. Whatever we allow into our mind affects our decisions (v23).
- Avoid anything that may tempt you to deceive others, tell lies or use your tongue to put others down (v24).
- Focus on Jesus. Ask yourself what He would want you to do. And ask yourself if you would be ashamed to take Him where you're going (v25).

Remember that Jesus has already walked that path you are on. He knows your worries and cares. God is with you and on your side!

 Think carefully about the route you're choosing and where it leads.

Take it all

'My son, do not forget my teaching, but keep my commands in your heart, for they will prolong your life many years and bring you peace and prosperity … Do not be wise in your own eyes; fear the LORD and shun evil. This will bring health to your body and nourishment to your bones … My son, do not despise the LORD's discipline, and do not resent his rebuke, because the LORD disciplines those he loves, as a father the son he delights in.' **PROVERBS 3:1–2,7–8,11–12**

God asks for, and deserves, one thing from us: our all! Wholehearted faith in God means giving over everything to Him – the good and the bad! We can trust Him with it and this sets us free to follow His way.

Sometimes, perhaps without realising, we pick and choose which parts of the Bible we believe in and which we don't feel are for us. But *all* of God's teaching and commands are meant for *all* of us, no exceptions.

It can be hard, there's no doubt about that, especially when we have to give up what we love so much, but **God gives back far more than we can give.** In today's reading He promises peace, prosperity, health and nourishment!

But most importantly He promises us that He loves and delights in us as our Father.

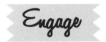 **God's love shows us that His commands are not a pick'n'mix. They are not a set of stuffy rules just put there to spoil our fun or set us up for failure. They were all made for a reason: God loves us so much, He doesn't want to see us come to any harm and He wants us to reach our full potential.**

Thank You, Lord, for Your commands and Your discipline in my life. You want only the best for me. Help me to live Your way, obeying all of Your teaching. Amen.

discipline

Who's First?

'Now the LORD God had planted a garden in the east, in Eden; and there he put the man he had formed. The LORD God made all kinds of trees grow out of the ground – trees that were pleasing to the eye and good for food. In the middle of the garden were the tree of life and the tree of the knowledge of good and evil. A river watering the garden flowed from Eden; from there it was separated into four headwaters … The LORD God took the man and put him in the Garden of Eden to work it and take care of it.'

GENESIS 2:8–10,15

Every day God gives us twenty-four hours to spend. It can be easy to rush around doing a million things and find that all of our time has been used up! Then, just as we're about to go to sleep, we suddenly realise, 'Oh no! I haven't spent any time with God! … Oh! … Er … Dear Lord … snore … snore …'

Living in paradise didn't mean Adam and Eve could splash on the sun lotion and take it easy. God didn't put them there as garden ornaments but to take charge of His creation. Without their gardening skills there would be disorder. And **without God's planning and guidance there would be chaos.**

We know how this story ends – with disobedience and so unfortunately, no more paradise.

God encourages us to take charge and make decisions but He is always around to give advice when we need it. These next few days we're going to explore the theme of priorities and see how people in the Bible had good, and sometimes bad, things at the top of their list. When time is so easily spent, let's learn how to spend it on what (and who!) really matters.

 God created us with thinking minds so that we could talk with Him and plan the best way to use our time and energy. By reading these notes and your Bible, and by praying, you're on the right track!

First things first

'In the first month of the first year of his reign, he opened the doors of the temple of the LORD and repaired them … Early the next morning King Hezekiah gathered the city officials together and went up to the temple of the LORD … Hezekiah gave the order to sacrifice the burnt offering on the altar. As the offering began, singing to the LORD began also, accompanied by trumpets and the instruments of David king of Israel. The whole assembly bowed in worship, while the musicians played and the trumpets sounded … So the service of the temple of the LORD was re-established.'

2 CHRONICLES 29:3,20,27–28,35

King Hezekiah inherited a complete mess when he succeeded his father, Ahaz. We read that Ahaz 'promoted wickedness' and 'had been most unfaithful to the LORD' (2 Chron. 28:19). Big mistake! And to add insult to injury 'Ahaz gathered together the furnishings from the temple of God and cut them in pieces. He shut the doors of the LORD's temple and set up altars at every street corner in Jerusalem. In every town in Judah he built high places to burn sacrifices to other gods and aroused the anger of the LORD' (2 Chron. 28:24–25).

He most certainly did not put God in His rightful place.

But it was Hezekiah's turn to reign and he didn't waste any time making things right! The very first day he took over, he scheduled a meeting with the Levites to get the nation worshipping God again. Within a fortnight the derelict Temple was back in operation. Hezekiah was up early the next morning, meeting with his officials to plan a great worship service. Everyone thanked God for the speed at which things were turned around.

Engage

Spend some time asking God if you, like Ahaz, are putting other things before Him. If anything springs to mind (perhaps you're more concerned with popularity than with pleasing God) then that's the Holy Spirit prompting you to the things that need to change. Ask God to help you be more like Hezekiah: putting Him first in everything. When God is Number One in your life, you'll find that everything else falls into place.

Work to do

'Go to the ant, you sluggard; consider its ways and be wise! It has no commander, no overseer or ruler, yet it stores its provisions in summer and gathers its food at harvest. How long will you lie there, you sluggard? When will you get up from your sleep? A little sleep, a little slumber, a little folding of the hands to rest – and poverty will come on you like a thief and scarcity like an armed man.'

PROVERBS 6:6–11

'*Sluggard*' is an old-fashioned name for someone who is a couch potato. King Solomon had little time for those who folded their arms instead of rolling up their sleeves. A lazy person is as much help as smoke in your eyes (Prov. 10:26). She wants, wants, wants, but won't give (13:4), makes excuses (22:13) and thinks it's cool to be laid back (26:16).

Ants, as small and insignificant as they seem, are actually sterling examples of how we should live. They don't shirk out of work. They don't need teacher ants to tell them to be quiet and get on, or leader ants to nag them into doing their bit. They all get on and work because if they don't NOW they won't have anything LATER.

God is with us NOW and He has amazing plans for each of us. **He wants to help you to live a dramatically different life** – befriending people who are usually ignored, speaking the truth when everyone else is lying, and maybe even performing miracles. But we need to do something too. We need to work at giving God time and space to be in our lives.

It takes work to let God run our lives. We need to talk with Him, ask His opinion on things, listen to His guidance, rely on His power and experience His love for us. But when we allow Him into our lives like that, we find that He is the One who actually does the real work.

Pray

Father, it's not always easy for me to let You be in charge of my life, but I want to learn how to! Please teach me. Amen.

Planning permission

'You see the trouble we are in: Jerusalem lies in ruins, and its gates have been burned with fire. Come, let us rebuild the wall of Jerusalem, and we will no longer be in disgrace … Let us start rebuilding … The God of heaven will give us success. We his servants will start rebuilding' **NEHEMIAH 2:17–18,20**

Nehemiah was given a huge civil engineering project – to rebuild the walls of Jerusalem. And he got it done in just fifty-two days (Neh. 6:15)! **He succeeded because he asked for God's help with every detail.** He made a plan and stuck to it. While others were resting he went on his own to look at the site. He travelled over two miles, examining foundations, the damage, and assessing work needing to be done. He did his planning late into the night so he wouldn't be seen. He wanted his plan to be fully worked out before he told anyone about it.

Nehemiah took God seriously and he took God's Word seriously. His main concern was to see God glorified in everything he did. If that is our concern too, then God will give our plans success.

So, if you need to draw up a plan, here's the failsafe way: spend time having a look at what needs to be done; work out the best way to get the project done; get started; trust that God will give you success!

God says we can talk through our plans with Him and He will help us. Are you struggling with a difficult project at the moment? Pray about it. Plan it. Start it. Keep praying. Keep going. Finish it. Praise God!

Pray

God, I thank You for giving me dreams and showing me what needs to be made better in the world around me. Please help me make the right plans so I can fulfil these dreams in the way You want. Be with me every step of the way. Amen.

dreams

Keep it up

'the LORD Almighty says: "Give careful thought to your ways. Go up into the mountains and bring down timber and build my house, so that I may take pleasure in it and be honoured … You expected much, but see, it turned out to be little. What you brought home, I blew away. Why? … Because of my house, which remains a ruin, while each of you is busy with your own house."' **HAGGAI 1:7–9**

What was it about keeping God's Temple in good order that the people found so hard?! Again we see it in ruins. One thing's for sure: **starting a job is one thing, finishing it is another.** When Zerubbabel, leader of the Jews, and Joshua the high priest, returned from exile in Persia, God told them to rebuild the Temple in Jerusalem.

After sorting out the Temple's foundations, Zerubbabel, Joshua and God's people gave up on the project for 18 years! All their efforts went into building luxury homes for themselves. They had plenty of excuses … too busy … not enough time … no one else is doing it … They just kept putting God's work off and off.

God told Haggai to tell them to think long and hard about their attitude. Their own foolish plans had no chance. They 'expected much' from their own way, but it 'turned out to be little' – nothing compared to God's way. Let's learn from their mistake!

 Engage

Sometimes it's really easy to get sidetracked and forget what God has asked you to do. Other things can often seem more appealing. As the Israelites learned, we need to keep our eyes fixed on God and on our destination, heaven. Jesus found it tough finishing the job God had given Him – going to the cross. So He talked about the problem and His feelings with His Father. Strengthened, He carried on until He was able to say, 'It is finished!'

keep on

Finished!

'Then Zerubbabel … Joshua … and the whole remnant of the people obeyed the voice of the LORD their God … And the people feared the LORD. Then Haggai, the LORD's messenger, gave this message of the LORD to the people: "I am with you," declares the LORD. So the LORD stirred up the spirit of Zerubbabel … Joshua … and the spirit of the whole remnant of the people. They came and began to work on the house of the LORD Almighty, their God' **HAGGAI 1:12–14**

Continuing on from the story of Zerubbabel and co, we see a turning point in today's reading. Finally the people obeyed the Lord and got on with rebuilding the Temple. They put their own dreams and plans to the side because they heard God's voice tell them what they should really be doing with the time He gave them. Perhaps we should remember, on a regular basis, to ask God how He thinks we're getting on. Ask, then be patient and listen for an answer, because He does and will give us guidance.

So what was it that got God's people working on the Temple again? Yes, God told them to do it, but they also needed something else to **motivate, energize**

and keep them persevering. What is it we need when we've got homework, revision, or a project at church to complete? We've all tried and failed many times when we do things in our own strength, because what we need is God to be with us. And He promises to be with us through His Holy Spirit.

 We need the Holy Spirit to help us stick with a job. All those characteristics we need to finish a challenging task – patience, peace, perseverance – come from God. So if you find it all too easy to opt out, ask God to keep you at it.

Pray

Lord God, help me to keep going with important tasks. Create in me the characteristics I need to finish them. Amen.

What's in it for me?

'May God, who has caused his Name to dwell there, overthrow any king or people who lifts a hand to change this decree or to destroy this temple in Jerusalem. I Darius have decreed it ... So the elders of the Jews continued to build and prosper under the preaching of Haggai the prophet and Zechariah, a descendant of Iddo. They finished building the temple according to the command of the God of Israel and the decrees of Cyrus, Darius and Artaxerxes, kings of Persia. The temple was completed on the third day of the month Adar, in the sixth year of the reign of King Darius. Then the people of Israel – the priests, the Levites and the rest of the exiles – celebrated the dedication of the house of God with joy.' **EZRA 6:12,14–16**

It took four years to rebuild the Temple. Four years of hard slog. Who got the applause at the end? Zerubbabel? Joshua the high priest? The workers? None of them get a mention. The credits roll for God.

Attitude counts! In their 'me first' mode, channeling their time and energy into building up a better lifestyle, the Jews ended up as down and outs. Once they put God first and made the Temple their priority, everything got better. They had food and all they needed!

Notice that they weren't in this for what they could get out of it. Zerubbabel wasn't expecting a medal. Joshua didn't ask for a statue of himself to be built in his memory. **They worked to bring glory to God.**

And that's what happened. The dedication of the Temple was a celebration of praise. Sacrifices were offered as people were challenged to live holy lives. Priests and Levites got themselves organised to teach right from wrong. People gave God their best and brought a nation back to Him!

Engage

What God starts He finishes. And He can help us get our work done well and on time! Towards the end of his life Paul could hold his head up and say, 'I have fought the good fight, I have finished the race, I have kept the faith' (2 Tim. 4:7). He had done God's work in God's way. What can you do well today to bring credit to God?

Busy bee

'As Jesus and his disciples were on their way, he came to a village where a woman named Martha opened her home to him. She had a sister called Mary, who sat at the Lord's feet listening to what he said. But Martha was distracted by all the preparations that had to be made. She came to him and asked, "Lord, don't you care that my sister has left me to do the work by myself? Tell her to help me!" "Martha, Martha," the Lord answered, "you are worried and upset about many things, but few things are needed – or indeed only one. Mary has chosen what is better, and it will not be taken away from her."' **LUKE 10:38–42**

On to another Bible story today and we meet up with Mary and Martha – two sisters who were good friends of Jesus. So Martha welcomes Jesus into her house. Imagine the privilege! But unfortunately for Martha, her 'to do list' is ridiculously long. Whereas her sister Mary had just one thing on hers: **spend time with Jesus.**

God wants us to give our best but He doesn't expect us to become frazzled, burnt-out workaholics. It's important to take time out to relax, to get to know other people and to worship God.

Martha put herself under unnecessary pressure, whipping up a five-course meal when a snack would have done. Her sister Mary was all for getting a take-away so they could spend more time with Jesus. Jesus pointed out that it was Mary, not Martha, who had taken the best option. The question wasn't who was working harder but who was using their time more wisely.

 If you are too busy for God then you are too busy. Chill out and find time for Him. No matter how pressurised you feel, you're always better off for reading your Bible and talking with Him. Try it!

Pray

Jesus, I want to spend more time at Your feet, just like Mary. I want to give You more time to teach me, to talk with me and just be with me. It's an amazing privilege! Thank You. Amen.

At your service

'the kingdom of heaven will be like ten virgins who took their lamps and went out to meet the bridegroom. Five of them were foolish and five were wise. The foolish ones took their lamps but did not take any oil with them. The wise ones, however, took oil in jars along with their lamps. The bridegroom was a long time in coming … The foolish ones said to the wise, "Give us some of your oil; our lamps are going out."

"No," they replied, "… go to those who sell oil and buy some for yourselves." But while they were on their way to buy the oil, the bridegroom arrived. The virgins who were ready went in with him to the wedding banquet. And the door was shut.' **MATTHEW 25:1–10**

Planning ahead is important if you want to make the most of opportunities. Around the time when Jesus told this parable, it was the custom for the bridegroom to travel to his bride's house and bring her back to his home for the wedding festivities. Imagine a camel with two white ribbons pulling up outside your house!

The bride, looking beautiful and smelling of the best perfumes, would leave her home with a crown on her head. Drummers and musicians would play a few 'Here comes the bride' numbers and guests would join in the procession along the route.

Part of the wedding was for guests to carry a lamp or torch. Without it they wouldn't be allowed to enter the bridegroom's home for the reception and dancing. You've heard of white weddings – these were light weddings!

The five guests who **missed out** had not planned ahead. The procession was delayed and their lamps ran out of oil.

 Engage

Those who drift on without planning ahead get caught out. Jesus told this parable so we would make the best use of our time before He returns. We can be wise, filled with His Spirit and shine for Him or flicker about, die out and hide in the darkness. Don't miss out!

Pray ....

Lord Jesus, help me to use my time wisely. Let me always be ready to serve You. Amen.

Ambition

'The ground of a certain rich man yielded an abundant harvest. He thought to himself, "What shall I do? I have no place to store my crops." Then he said, "This is what I'll do. I will tear down my barns and build bigger ones, and there I will store my surplus grain. And I'll say to myself, 'You have plenty of grain laid up for many years. Take life easy; eat, drink and be merry.'" But God said to him, "You fool! This very night your life will be demanded from you. Then who will get what you have prepared for yourself?" This is how it will be with whoever stores up things for themselves but is not rich towards God.' **LUKE 12:16–21**

If you want to be a brain surgeon your goal this year might be to improve in biology. If you want to be a train spotter your goal might be saving up for a new anorak. If you want to be a dancer your goal may very well be getting some lessons. Everyone sets goals. You've probably been made to do it at school: 'My goal is to get to lessons on time.' Well, seeing as it's something we all do let's listen to the important things Jesus has to say about the goals we set.

It's a good idea to set ourselves goals. Without them we become aimless and unprepared for the future. So when does ambition become a foolish thing? The answer lies in whether we're walking closely with God and listening to His ambition for our lives, or, we're listening to our own selfish desires – I want to be rich, successful, respected, secure, etc. **Are we storing things up for ourselves or adding to the kingdom of God?**

 'Fools!' That's what Jesus says of those who spend their time living to fulfill selfish ambitions. It's not wrong to be ambitious. Jesus said we should aim to become rich – in our relationship with Him. Are you investing time to have a bigger and better friendship with Jesus?

Lord Jesus, thank You that You want me to succeed and fulfill my potential. Please guide me towards the correct goals and make sure that knowing You better is always my top priority. Amen.

Talent search

'it will be like a man going on a journey, who called his servants and entrusted his wealth to them. To one he gave five bags of gold ... Then he went on his journey. The man who had received five bags of gold went at once and put his money to work and gained five bags more ... After a long time the master of those servants returned and settled accounts with them. The man who had received five bags of gold brought the other five. "Master," he said, "you entrusted me with five bags of gold. See, I have gained five more." His master replied, "Well done, good and faithful servant! You have been faithful with a few things; I will put you in charge of many things. Come and share your master's happiness!"'

MATTHEW 25:14–16,19–21

Are you making good use of your gifts and abilities for Jesus? This particular servant had the right idea. **He used his gift to gain more for his master.** How do we use our gifts to gain more for God? Perhaps if we're good at singing we could lead more people into worshipping God. Or maybe we're good with kids and teaching. Why not use this skill to teach at Sunday school? You'd be adding to the kingdom by helping raise up the next generation! Or perhaps you're good at hospitality – there's nothing better for a new person attending church than to be welcomed and given a hot, delicious cup of coffee!

So ask God to help you develop your talents and earn the big 'Well done!' Also remember, you need to use your talents as God asks you to, and not just to please others.

 Another servant in this story buried his 'talent'. Perhaps it was because he saw that he was only given one while the other two servants where given more, and so he didn't feel good enough. Do you ever feel like that? Like you've drawn the short straw? Well, don't! Your talents are just as important as any others because God gave them to you. Be thankful for them and put them to good use!

Father, thank You for the gifts and skills You've given me. Show me how to use them wisely. Amen.

Chill out

'Submit to God and be at peace with him; in this way prosperity will come to you. Accept instruction from his mouth and lay up his words in your heart. If you return to the Almighty, you will be restored … Surely then you will find delight in the Almighty and will lift up your face to God. You will pray to him, and he will hear you, and you will fulfil your vows. What you decide on will be done, and light will shine on your ways. When people are brought low and you say, "Lift them up!" then he will save the downcast. He will deliver even one who is not innocent, who will be delivered through the cleanness of your hands.'

JOB 22:21–30

Rest and relaxation are important! There *is* a time to crash out on the sofa. Life can get pretty wild. There's so much noise … TV, sound system, raised voices, traffic. There's so much to do. Stop, world, I want to get off!

Job felt like that. Everywhere he looked he could see problems. His home life, his family life, his work life – his whole life – were full of hassles and pressure.

He could hardly cope. And it wasn't fair. What had he done to deserve this hassle? He was overstretched to snapping point. So Eliphaz dished out this advice:

Take time out to find God's peace ...

- read what God has to say and be built up …
- pray to God because He listens …
- be humble and ask God to show you the next move …
- allow God to deliver you from the pressures you are under.

At the beginning or end of a busy day, Jesus would often disappear up into the mountains for some peace and quiet. He would take His disciples away from the crowds to relax and wind down. It's good for us to be active, but it's also important to find time to be alone with God. He can keep your life full of peace and in one piece!

Work and play

'Three times a year you are to celebrate a festival to me. Celebrate the Festival of Unleavened Bread; for seven days eat bread made without yeast, as I commanded you. Do this at the appointed time in the month of Aviv, for in that month you came out of Egypt. No one is to appear before me empty-handed. Celebrate the Festival of Harvest with the firstfruits of the crops you sow in your field. Celebrate the Festival of Ingathering at the end of the year, when you gather in your crops from the field. Three times a year all the men are to appear before the Sovereign LORD.'

EXODUS 23:14–17

Holidays and celebrations were God's idea. In today's reading we see God planned a festival for His people. **He made us with a need for relaxing and having fun.** For singing, dancing and enjoying good food! For meeting up with family and friends. And as Christians we have so much to be joyful and thankful for:

- The Creator of the universe made each of us with a *lot* of care

- God sent His Son to show us how to live life to the full
- Jesus died for us so that we could be forgiven
- We get to spend eternity with God in paradise
- God loves us!

Can you think of any more reasons to thank God? Add them to your prayers today.

Engage **Ask God to remind you to make the most of your spare time by celebrating and relaxing. He knows how to make our time into a really good time!**

Pray

Lord, I thank You that holidays and celebrations are in Your plan for our lives. Help me to really enjoy these fun and relaxing times spent with the ones I love – including You! Amen.

play

God's time

'Do you not know? Have you not heard? The LORD is the everlasting God, the Creator of the ends of the earth. He will not grow tired or weary, and his understanding no one can fathom. He gives strength to the weary and increases the power of the weak. Even youths grow tired and weary, and young men stumble and fall; but those who hope in the LORD will renew their strength. They will soar on wings like eagles; they will run and not grow weary, they will walk and not be faint.' **ISAIAH 40:28–31**

We all get tired and feel weary, but God promises to lift us up and give us strength if we put first things first, and hope in Him. Let's look at the way God uses His time for us.

Does God take time off? No way! Looking after His family is a full-time job. God doesn't need a holiday or an occasional weekend off. His mind is alive and alert twenty-four hours a day. His ability to deal with us is amazing. His understanding is incredible. And He loves us so much! As for wearing Him down – no chance.

So how does God spend His time? God gives His power to those on their knees. He revives those who have taken knocks. He gives strength to those who are feeling weak. Whether it is weakness to temptation or weakness through ill health, God comes along and builds us up or puts us back together. **He is always ready and waiting to give us His time.** Will we accept the offer?

Eagles are able to soar up and up. And the higher they go the smaller the world and all its problems become. Those who spend time with God don't need to be squashed with pressures. He is able to lift you out of your worries and above your problems. God has given all His time over to looking after you. Take time to thank Him.

God, thank You for being my wings and lifting me up. Never let me stop having faith in You. Amen.

Heart Clear Out

'There are six things the LORD hates, seven that are detestable to him: haughty eyes, a lying tongue, hands that shed innocent blood, a heart that devises wicked schemes, feet that are quick to rush into evil, a false witness who pours out lies and a person who stirs up conflict in the community.' **PROVERBS 6:16–19**

Just as we can be a bit slack in keeping our bedrooms tidy, **our hearts can fill up with all sorts of rubbish,** and before we know it we're hoarding things that are dirty and rotting. Yuk! And just as our mums would give us a 'kind' reminder to sort it out, the Bible and the Holy Spirit will give us the kick we need to clean up our hearts. 'A good man brings good things out of the good stored up in his heart, and an evil man brings evil things out of the evil stored up in his heart' (Luke 6:45).

So in this section we're going to explore what might be the 'dirty and rotting' things in our hearts and this verse is a good place to start! All of these things God hates originate from our heart. For example, 'the mouth speaks what the heart is full of' (Luke 6:45) so it is our hearts which decide to lie first, then our mouths follow. This is why the Bible says, 'Above all else, guard your heart, for everything you do flows from it' (Prov. 4:23).

As we look at a few possible flaws in our hearts, we're going to see what the Bible says we can do about them. And very helpfully it has some top advice on all of it!

Are you ready for a heart clear out? Let's go!

Pray

> *Holy Spirit, You are our greatest help for*
> *sorting out our hearts. You can show us*
> *the areas that need changing. Please fill*
> *me now and be with me every day. Amen.*

Too much!

'If you find honey, eat just enough –
too much of it, and you will vomit …
The greedy stir up conflict, but those
who trust in the LORD will prosper.'

PROVERBS 25:16; 28:25

Why is it when we get what we want, we always
want more? And some people cause all kinds of trouble
to get more than their fair share of anything. Greed
may sound like need but there is a world of difference
between them.

Have you ever sat and stuffed your face with your
favourite food until you felt ill? Solomon says that
honey tastes great in small doses but if you eat it by the
bucketful it will make you sick.

When we grab more than our fair share of anything it
has harmful consequences. It's not that honey is bad for
you. It's the quantity that's the problem. There's nothing
wrong with money but when we're greedy for the latest
and greatest it can lead us into all kinds of problems.

It's the same with all our desires. It's good to have
confidence but too much and we get conceited. It's good
to care about your appearance but when you spend
hours preening in front of a mirror you can become vain.

Greed turns the good things in life into the bad things in life. The exception is Jesus. You can never get enough of Him.

Living life to the full doesn't mean we need to fill our lives to the full. God isn't interested in what we have but who we are. Learn to value Jesus and the value He places on you, so you will enjoy the sweet things in life without getting sick.

Dear Lord, please help me to see when I am being greedy, whether it be with money, possessions, popularity or self-confidence. You are the only one who truly satisfies! I need more of You. Amen.

Green-eyed monster

'My son, if your heart is wise, then my heart will be glad indeed; my inmost being will rejoice when your lips speak what is right. Do not let your heart envy sinners, but always be zealous for the fear of the LORD. There is surely a future hope for you, and your hope will not be cut off. Listen, my son, and be wise, and set your heart on the right path: do not join those who drink too much wine or gorge themselves on meat, for drunkards and gluttons become poor, and drowsiness clothes them in rags ... A heart at peace gives life to the body, but envy rots the bones.' **PROVERBS 23:15–21; 14:30**

Jealousy chews away at us, getting more and more serious by the day. The sort of jealousy in our reading today happens when our Christian life no longer seems to have all the answers. We may look around and think our non-Christian friends have got a better deal in life. Maybe they have more friends, even more fun.

If we get into thinking this way, we ought to remember three things:

1. Jesus never promised Christians an easy life.
2. We have a great privilege in knowing God as our Father, who gives us everything we need and will be with us whatever we face. **We have no need to be jealous,** because in Jesus we have everything that is good for us.
3. The things God is working on in our lives will go on forever, not just a little while.

One of the secrets of happiness is learning to be content with the things God has given us. Appreciate the things God has brought to your life and tell Him how thankful you are.

Pray

Dear God, thank You for giving me so many good things. Amen.

What goes up must come down

'The LORD detests all the proud of heart. Be sure of this: they will not go unpunished ... Pride goes before destruction, a haughty spirit before a fall. Better to be lowly in spirit along with the oppressed than to share plunder with the proud. Whoever gives heed to instruction prospers, and blessed is the one who trusts in the LORD ... Haughty eyes and a proud heart – the unploughed field of the wicked – produce sin ... Pride brings a person low, but the lowly in spirit gain honour.' **PROVERBS 16:5,18–20; 21:4; 29:23**

God's way is often the opposite to the way of our culture. For example, many idolise celebrities, believing them to be 'more important' because of their status. But this is not God's way – don't go with this flow! God does not care for status. God cares about our hearts.

All through the Bible are stories of God using the lowest of the low, the outsiders and the 'weak' to do amazing things for Him, because He saw through to their hearts and He recognised their humility.

So when you are taking out the bins or mopping the floor, remember, God sees you and your humble work for Him and He's going to use you for good things. It's Him you need to impress, no one else. Don't fall into the status trap; don't think you are less important than those in the spotlight.

The real problem with pride is that it gives us such big heads that we think we don't need God – 'don't worry, God, I've got this'. But humble people know the truth. **We need God for everything.** We are nothing without Him.

Just get your mind around the humility of Jesus for a moment. He gave up everything to become a servant and die on the cross (Phil. 2:5–8). You can't get more humble than that. But the result of hitting the lowest point of humility was the reward of the ultimate top spot – 'the name that is above every name' (Phil. 2:9).

Only skin deep

'She is worth far more than rubies … She brings … good, not harm all the days of her life … She sets about her work vigorously; her arms are strong for her tasks. She sees that her trading is profitable, and her lamp does not go out at night … She opens her arms to the poor and extends her hands to the needy … She is clothed with strength and dignity; she can laugh at the days to come. She speaks with wisdom, and faithful instruction is on her tongue … Charm is deceptive, and beauty is fleeting; but a woman who fears the LORD is to be praised. Honour her for all that her hands have done, and let her works bring her praise' **PROVERBS 31:10,12, 17–18,20,25–26,30–31**

Leading on from the topic of pride, today's heart issue is: vanity. How much time do we spend each day looking in the mirror and scrutinizing our appearance? Perhaps you absolutely *love* your reflection or maybe you avoid a mirror at all costs!

Being positively/negatively obsessed with our looks to the point where our confidence and self-esteem are influenced by them, and not God, is dangerous ground. It's like building a house on sand. **We're used to the idea that outer beauty is to be praised,** but the Bible tells us that something else is worth a lot more: our character.

What are we like when no one's watching? Do we help that person others ignore? Do we put all our effort into a task we've been given? And most importantly, do we fear the Lord? To fear God is to respect Him by following His ways and obeying Him, not to hide from Him or be scared like it may sound. If we 'fear God' then all these other good character traits will come to us. This is what makes our hearts beautiful – a beauty which doesn't fade!

 Engage

If you struggle with low confidence and self-esteem talk to God about it now. He wants you to know how amazingly special and unique you are; how much you are worth to Him. And whenever a negative thought comes to you, or a memory of something nasty said about you, choose to call it out for what it is – a lie – and don't believe it!

Wound up

'The wise fear the LORD and shun evil, but a fool is hotheaded and yet feels secure. A quick-tempered person does foolish things, and the one who devises evil schemes is hated ... Whoever is patient has great understanding, but one who is quick-tempered displays folly ... A hot-tempered person stirs up conflict, but the one who is patient calms a quarrel.'

PROVERBS 14:16–17,29; 15:18

How do you react when someone gets on your nerves? Even our best friends can wind us up at times. Whether they say something nasty or do something irritating, we can quickly reach boiling point and lash out without thinking of the damage. But going into nuclear meltdown and shouting at them is like throwing paraffin onto a bonfire – it's likely to flare up out of control.

When we're annoyed, even provoked, it is better to think before speaking. A gentle answer or a kind act is like pouring water on the flames. Sometimes it is best not to say anything at all until you've calmed down. **Words spoken in anger can leave scars.**

People often remember the few horrible things said about them over the hundreds of nice things. So hold back and get some space, before you make a mistake and a fool of yourself.

If cross words have been spoken remember the cross that Jesus died on. Ask the forgiveness of those you have hurt. Forgive them too, and ask God to forgive you. Get arguments settled fast!

 Has someone you know been really winding you up lately? Are you being tempted to hate someone? It may even be someone who's close to you, such as a friend or family member. Ask God to help you cope and also to help you love that person, or those people. Pray and prepare for a miracle!

Father God, please keep all hatred away from me and bless those who are making my life difficult at the moment. I pray that You will keep me safe and that they will soon know Your love for them. Amen.

Use with care

'Whoever conceals hatred with lying lips and spreads slander is a fool. Sin is not ended by multiplying words, but the prudent hold their tongues. The tongue of the righteous is choice silver, but the heart of the wicked is of little value. The lips of the righteous nourish many, but fools die for lack of sense ... Evildoers are trapped by their sinful talk ... An honest witness tells the truth, but a false witness tells lies. The words of the reckless pierce like swords, but the tongue of the wise brings healing. Truthful lips endure for ever, but a lying tongue lasts only a moment ... Those who guard their lips preserve their lives, but those who speak rashly will come to ruin.'

PROVERBS 10:18–21; 12:13,17–19; 13:3

These are wise words about unwise words. Have you heard the proverb, 'Sticks and stones may break my bones, but words will never harm me'? How untrue is this! Words do hurt. And the effects can last and last. That's why this proverb is not in the Bible and Solomon wouldn't agree with it.

Words have electrifying power. A lie, an insult, a bit of gossip, a swear word, negative advice: they can cause devastation not only to the victim but also to the one who uses them. And it's dangerously easy to slip into these bad habits. So let's make a change.

Think before you speak. Use the mouth God gave you to say things that would please Him. It's wise to say things that build friendships – kind words, appreciative comments, compliments, genuine concern. These kinds of words bring life not ruin. Just as obeying our parents comes with the promise of longer life, so guarding our lips protects life.

Engage Our world has a serious shortage of kind, thoughtful words. Ask God to help you remember that today and do your bit to help solve this problem.

Pray

Father, please help me to speak kind, caring, encouraging words. Amen.

Did you hear …?

'Without wood a fire goes out; without a gossip a quarrel dies down. As charcoal to embers and as wood to fire, so is a quarrelsome person for kindling strife. The words of a gossip are like choice morsels; they go down to the inmost parts. Like a coating of silver dross on earthenware are fervent lips with an evil heart. Enemies disguise themselves with their lips, but in their hearts they harbour deceit. Though their speech is charming, do not believe them, for seven abominations fill their hearts. Their malice may be concealed by deception, but their wickedness will be exposed in the assembly. Whoever digs a pit will fall into it; if someone rolls a stone, it will roll back on them. A lying tongue hates those it hurts, and a flattering mouth works ruin.' **PROVERBS 26:20–28**

Gossip spreads like wildfire and, like Chinese whispers, it distorts truth, and escalates until there is not an ounce of truth left. And you never really learn from this mistake until the gossip is about you!

Let's get wise to the damage gossip does to others and also to those who gossip. Proverbs pulls no punches about the kind of people who spread malicious gossip. On the surface they look charming and lovely, but it only disguises the darkness and deceit in their hearts. Those who are keen to spread gossip often do so out of envy. They foolishly think that by denting other people's reputations they will improve theirs. But they roll out a stone that'll roll back on them.

The wise way is to **make yourself the end link of any gossip chain.** Don't pass on the unfair, unkind or unproven remarks you hear about others. When possible, avoid listening to gossip in the first place because it only fuels quarrels.

 Proverbs 26 takes the lid off gossip by exposing it as the colourful front that masks hatred and envy. Think of gossip as a means of propelling hatred and you begin to wise up to the damage it can do. Ask God to focus your mind on things that are true, honest, lovely and pure.

Hold fire

HEART
CLEAR OUT

'Starting a quarrel is like breaching a dam; so drop the matter before a dispute breaks out … Whoever loves a quarrel loves sin; whoever builds a high gate invites destruction … A person's wisdom yields patience; it is to one's glory to overlook an offence … Like one who grabs a stray dog by the ears is someone who rushes into a quarrel not their own.'

PROVERBS 17:14,19; 19:11; 26:17

An argument can cause a lot of damage, like breaching a dam, so here are some key tips for avoiding fights:

1. Don't get involved in an argument between other people. Chipping in your opinion when it's not sought can only make matters worse. **Perhaps leave the scene entirely** if you feel you could cut in at any second.

2. When someone winds you up, don't hit back with your words. We've looked briefly before at the effects of our words and it's not pretty. Take it on the chin and be bigger than they are by ignoring them or walking away.

3. If you disagree with someone over any matter, don't stand your ground and fight it out till one of you gives in. If the matter looks as if it'll boil over into a quarrel, drop it ... even if you know you are right. What's the point in winning an argument but losing a friend? That doesn't mean you shouldn't have strong opinions or listen to those who think differently to you, but once the talk becomes overcharged with pride, tempers can flare.

Engage

'Do not say, "I'll do to them as they have done to me; I'll pay them back for what they did"' (Prov. 24:29). You can't argue with that, can you? If you have been hot-headed with someone lately, put the matter right. Ask God to help you express your opinions and feelings without giving offence.

feelings

The whole truth

'To you, O people, I call out; I raise my voice to all humanity. You who are simple, gain prudence; you who are foolish, set your hearts on it. Listen, for I have trustworthy things to say; I open my lips to speak what is right. My mouth speaks what is true, for my lips detest wickedness. All the words of my mouth are just; none of them is crooked or perverse. To the discerning all of them are right; they are upright to those who have found knowledge. Choose my instruction instead of silver, knowledge rather than choice gold, for wisdom is more precious than rubies, and nothing you desire can compare' **PROVERBS 8:4–11**

God is the God of truth, so it makes sense that we too should always be truthful in what we say. But we're not always, are we? Whether it's a little white lie to get us out of doing something we don't fancy, or a huge lie to get us out of major trouble, these are all pushing us into the 'crooked/perverse' category and out of the 'right/true' group.

We've probably all experienced the stress caused by trying to cover up a lie. We may go on telling more lies to keep the first from being discovered! It's pretty uncomfortable being called out on lying and it's almost guaranteed that, eventually, we will be.

So let's choose to be truthful. There are two mega important reasons to do so. The first is that 'the truth will set you free' (John 8:32)! Lies bind us up and give the devil the perfect opportunity to come in and mess things up.

The second reason is that truth makes things right. **Someone is always losing out when lies are involved.** Just think of a court case. If witnesses didn't tell the truth, the whole truth, and nothing but the truth, people could get away with terrible crimes and victims wouldn't receive justice.

Jesus said, 'I am … the truth' (John 14:6). And we need His help to keep us speaking only the truth and what is good. Here are three wise questions to ask before you speak. Is it helpful? Is it right? Is it true?

Jesus, please help me to be aware of when I'm using my mouth to speak negative or false words. Give me the courage to always tell the truth and say what is right. Amen.

Unshaken

'Keep me safe, my God, for in you I take refuge. I say to the LORD, "You are my Lord; apart from you I have no good thing." … LORD, you alone are my portion and my cup; you make my lot secure. The boundary lines have fallen for me in pleasant places; surely I have a delightful inheritance. I will praise the LORD, who counsels me; even at night my heart instructs me. I keep my eyes always on the LORD. With him at my right hand, I shall not be shaken.' **PSALM 16:1–2,5–8**

Life is not always super easy, is it? We can sometimes face major tragedies that make us question our faith in God. Perhaps the very fact we're a Christian makes life hard sometimes, with people picking on us, interrogating or judging us. Our faith will go through trials and tests and will be knocked. But these negative situations do not have to have negative outcomes. Our faith can indeed come out the other end even stronger. So how do we remain unshaken?

Well, the key thing is to **base your faith on truth, not on your feelings.** Sometimes we feel low and uninspired for no apparent reason, it just happens, doesn't it? Or sometimes a circumstance can make us feel anxious, scared, stressed, angry or sad.

If we base our faith on these feelings, it will be just as sensitive and unreliable.

So what does it mean to base our faith on truth? What is truth? We saw in the last day of 'Heart Clear Out' that God is truth (read John 1:1,14; 14:6). Everything God says in the Bible is the truth: every loving and guiding word. What Jesus did on the cross is the truth, from dying for our sins to defeating the grave. This is the truth! And the great thing about the truth is, unlike our feelings, it is as solid as a rock: it never ever changes, becomes less true or loses relevance to our lives.

 If you are going through a testing time at the moment, try not to focus on your feelings but focus completely on God and His Word. You may *feel* **that God is distant, but the** *truth* **is He is 'at [your] right hand'!**

Pray

Lord God, You are truth! Teach me to lean on You, not on my emotions. I pray You would help me, as I read more about unshaken faith, to really take on board these truths so that I can use them my whole life! Amen.

In God's hands

'Then Jacob called for his sons and said: "Gather round so that I can tell you what will happen to you in days to come … Joseph is a fruitful vine … his bow remained steady, his strong arms stayed supple, because of the hand of the Mighty One of Jacob, because of the Shepherd, the Rock of Israel, because of your father's God, who helps you, because of the Almighty, who blesses you … Let all these rest on the head of Joseph, on the brow of the prince among his brothers."' **GENESIS 49:1,22–26**

When Jacob was fed the lie that his favourite son, Joseph, had been torn to pieces by a ferocious animal, it really choked him up. He wasn't to know that Joseph was heading south, not west, having been sold as a slave into Egypt.

Jacob was inconsolable.

He likened his experience to going through hell (Sheol – Gen. 37:35). People still describe bad experiences as hellish. What they mean is that they can't see anything good or positive in what they are going through. They often think that God is not there or that He doesn't care.

Later Jacob was able to look back and see that **God had been in control of events after all.** The Lord hadn't stopped caring. He'd protected Joseph just like a shepherd guards his sheep. And He proved to be the Mighty One, Jacob's Rock – solid and reliable.

What a happy reunion there was many years later. Jacob was able to throw his arms around his long-lost son and weep tears of joy. It was one of the longest hugs in history (Gen. 46:29).

Jacob didn't get bitter about the way his other sons had almost sent him to an early grave. He gave them his blessing. But his blessing for Joseph just overflowed with praise. The Lord was his Helper! And the sourness tasted sweet.

Engage

It's hard to find God in the darker moments in life. But He is always there! We need to know that as a fact because when the heat is on, negative feelings can fry our faith. Sadness and hurt can chew up our love for God. We may not be able to thank Him for our troubles but we can always thank Him in our troubles. He's our Shepherd, our Rock and our Helper. He knows how to mend a broken heart.

For our good

'I will proclaim the name of the LORD. Oh, praise the greatness of our God! He is the Rock, his works are perfect, and all his ways are just. A faithful God who does no wrong, upright and just is he.'

DEUTERONOMY 32:3–4

Moses messed up. The consequence was: he couldn't enter the promised land. But he didn't bite back or spit out how unfairly God had treated him. He knew he had been out of order and had got what he deserved. Instead he told everyone (the whole nation was lined up) that God is great! And His greatness is to be praised. He learnt that in tough times the Lord is our Rock – solid and reliable.

Moses also learnt that **God only disciplines us because He loves us.** If we disobey there is a price to pay. And although being sorted out by God is never a comfortable experience, it's always for our good.

When we are disobedient, there are often messy stains to clear up or live with. It's no use trying to pin the blame on God or someone else. And by admitting his foolishness, Moses was a bigger and better man for it.

Moses warned others not to get an appetite for things God has kept off the menu. Sin may look good and taste good but don't be fooled into thinking it is good. God knows what's going on and will bring it up sooner or later.

 Engage

God is fair! He's perfect and He's right! God's not to blame for our failures. But He's good enough to help us out of the messes we get ourselves into. He points out the bad fruit in our lives because He has good fruit on offer. And He can take away the bad taste of disobedience that sometimes lingers. Ask for His forgiveness. Praise His greatness. Taste and see that the Lord is good.

good

All things are possible

'When the princes in Israel take the lead, when the people willingly offer themselves – praise the LORD! Hear this, you kings! Listen, you rulers! I, even I, will sing to the LORD; I will praise the LORD, the God of Israel, in song.' **JUDGES 5:2–3**

Deborah, a humble prophetess, had been appointed by God to lead the Israelites back to Him – and into battle. And the odds were stacked against her. Sisera had high-tech chariots. Deborah's troops under the leadership of Barak were armed with wooden farming implements. But **she was a tough cookie and decided to lead on because God was with her.**

It seemed impossible to take on those chariots but God had sent a rainstorm to flood the valley. The enemy were totally bogged down and defeated.

Deborah was the first to give God the credit. She didn't get bigheaded about her own ability. She was out to praise the Lord and celebrate His victory.

This is her victory song! It was a no-hope situation but the people willingly offered themselves to God. And God delivered them! That's why she couldn't help singing to Him!

Engage

Sometimes when we're in a tough situation, it's amazing to see how God can work. Deborah didn't complain about how unfair the situation was but quietly trusted God to overcome the problem. The hardest part wasn't fighting the enemy but surrendering to God. It's never easy to admit that God knows best when the situation looks worse. But Deborah trusted that God would take on the situation and all they had to do was follow Him. And she was right! Your battles are the Lord's battles. Follow Him and you'll see His power at work.

Pray

Dear God, when I face situations that seem impossible, remind me of Your awesome power that makes all things possible – I do not need to be afraid. Amen.

Look for the good

'A gazelle lies slain on your heights, Israel. How the mighty have fallen! ... Saul and Jonathan – in life they were loved and admired, and in death they were not parted. They were swifter than eagles, they were stronger than lions. Daughters of Israel, weep for Saul'

2 SAMUEL 1:19,23–24

David could have made a meal of Saul's downfall. After all, Saul had made his life a misery, hounding him into hiding and threatening his life. But instead David mourned him.

No matter how unfairly people treat you, it's not right to gloat when they get their just desserts. The mighty Saul had fallen but **David didn't have a bad word to say about him** – in private or public. Neither did David want the Philistines jeering and sneering at Saul. David knew Saul's weak points – his insecurities, jealously and temper that made him a bully. But not a word is mentioned of them in this lament.

Instead David sings about Saul's good points … his love and graciousness. He pays tribute to Saul's swiftness and strength. And he weeps for his fallen enemy.

It probably took more courage to say those kind things about Saul than it did to take on Goliath. And by doing so David showed why he was a man 'after God's own heart' (Acts 13:22).

When others brew up trouble for us, our first reaction is to hit back somehow. That's not Jesus' way. He came up with the expression 'turn the other cheek'. Not as a sign of weakness but a sign of strength – inner strength. Jesus didn't bad-mouth those who insulted Him. He forgave those who made Him suffer. He prayed for His enemies.

So instead of hurting those who get on the wrong side of you, help them instead. Look for their good points not their bad. Talk to God about them. His power at work in you will help you do what might seem impossible.

Facing fear

'He reached down from on high and took hold of me; he drew me out of deep waters. He rescued me from my powerful enemy, from my foes, who were too strong for me. They confronted me in the day of my disaster, but the LORD was my support. He brought me out into a spacious place; he rescued me because he delighted in me.' **2 SAMUEL 22:17–20**

It's not easy to cope with being around people who intimidate or bully us. The fear of what they may say or do next can overwhelm us and even push us into hiding. David certainly didn't enjoy living under threat – real or imagined. He vividly describes drowning in fear, 'waves of destruction' swirling about him, 'torrents of destruction' overwhelming him. Perhaps a situation you've been in has made you feel like this: sinking fast in fear.

So what did David do? The natural reaction to a threat is flight or fight. But David held his nerve and prayed. And he knew God had heard his cry.

Read David's description of God's power in 2 Samuel 22: 8–16. God is awesome! No one can get the better of Him. And **the moment David fills his mind with God, his fears disappear** and he bursts into praise. So when you're facing fear, remember:

- **God reaches.** Even if you're sinking He can get you (v17).
- **God rescues.** No matter how desperate the situation, God can help (v18).
- **God resuscitates.** He cares for you and gets you back on your feet (vv19–20).

Engage

David looked on God as being his fortress. When under threat he ran to God for protection. And Almighty God proved to be all mighty.

Pray

Lord, You are my fortress. I want to keep praising You, even when life gets hard. Amen.

protection

Don't worry

'the LORD says … "He will not enter this city or shoot an arrow here. He will not come before it with shield or build a siege ramp against it. By the way that he came he will return; he will not enter this city ... I will defend this city and save it, for my sake and for the sake of David my servant."' **2 KINGS 19:32–34**

Sennacherib, the king of Assyria, taunted Hezekiah by saying that God wouldn't bother to rescue him (19:10). And then boasted about the damage he had inflicted on other cities.

When we're under pressure it's often harder to trust in God. Doubts as to whether God really cares about us can consume our thoughts. And when there's trouble every way you turn, you can feel quite on your own.

Hezekiah knew what to do. He went up to the Temple and told God about the pressures he was under. He shared with God the insulting remarks of the Assyrians and asked God to deliver them. Not so he could sleep easier, but to teach the Assyrians to respect God.

Isaiah delivered God's reply. None of the things troubling Hezekiah would happen. Not a shot would be fired at Jerusalem. That night an angel of the Lord made mincemeat of the Assyrians and they retreated to Nineveh. And it was Sennacherib, not Hezekiah, who became history.

Engage Most of the things we worry about won't ever happen. Jesus told us that getting anxious about tomorrow won't help one bit. The important thing is to put God first in your life and let Him take care of the future (Matt. 6:33). God wants you to know that you are important to Him. So if you're troubled by anything, talk it through with Him.

When things fall apart

'Don't call me Naomi,' she told them. 'Call me Mara, because the Almighty has made my life very bitter. I went away full, but the LORD has brought me back empty. Why call me Naomi? The LORD has afflicted me; the Almighty has brought misfortune upon me.' **RUTH 1:20–21**

Life wasn't going well for Naomi. First there had been a famine. Then there had been an unwelcome house move to Moab. Then her husband died. To make matters worse her recently married sons died soon afterwards. When she arrived back in Bethlehem there was grief and despair written all over her face.

A series of tragedies had brought much suffering into Naomi's life. Deep down she may have had regrets about going to Moab. She may have thought somehow she was to blame. But she told everyone it was God's fault. She blamed God for her poverty, loneliness and suffering. And she felt very angry inside.

Deep suffering causes us to wonder if God really loves us. All kinds of negative thoughts can rise up. Is God punishing me for something I've done wrong? If God really cared why would He let me suffer like this?

Self-pity can lead to deep depression. Bitterness can poison our attitudes and alienate us from others. And it's difficult to appreciate or praise God when we feel sour.

Naomi couldn't see at the time how **God was putting her life back together.** First of all her daughter-in-law Ruth had chosen to stay with her. She wasn't alone. And Ruth worked extra hard to provide her with food and shelter.

Instead of becoming a lonely down-and-out she became a grandmother. Ruth married a rich landowner called Boaz and Naomi acted as nanny. Mara became Naomi again. God had taken away the bitterness.

Engage

Anger, resentment, guilt and crazy mixed-up feelings that God's got it in for you need to be sorted and removed from your life – and this is work for the Holy Spirit. Don't blame God when things don't work out. Get close and ask Him to take the sourness out of your attitude.

tragedy

God, I have a complaint

'I will not keep silent; I will speak out in the anguish of my spirit, I will complain in the bitterness of my soul … I despise my life; I would not live for ever. Let me alone; my days have no meaning.' **JOB 7:11,16**

Job suffered immense tragedy in his life. Once, he had everything going for him. Nice wife, big family, successful business, good health. He loved the Lord and obeyed Him. He found it easy because everything was working out fine. But then his business went bankrupt and his family were killed in a tragic accident. **He was deeply upset and shaken, but he turned to God not against Him** (Job 1:21).

Then came more suffering. He lost his good health. His grief was so intense he couldn't speak to anyone for a week. He was hardly recognisable.

Job couldn't understand why his life turned so bad. Why couldn't he get any peace? Or sleep? He had reached the point where he thought life wasn't worth living.

And his so-called friends weren't helping matters by making out that God must be punishing him for something he had done wrong. The last thing Job needed was to feel guilt, amongst all the other emotions. And the reality was that he hadn't done anything wrong.

Wisely Job didn't bottle up his feelings but told God exactly how he felt. He prayed an angry, bitter, complaining prayer, punctuated with 'whys': Why aren't things getting better? Why are You allowing this to happen to me? Why don't You tell me what I've done to deserve this?

Engage

God is there for our 'why' questions. He listened to Job and let him pour out his feelings. And if you are upset about anything, He wants you to tell Him all about it. Many of the prayers in the Bible are cries of distress. They were spoken in times of turmoil. God takes our complaints seriously and lovingly deals with them – and us!

Pray

Dear God, thank You for always listening to my prayers, even if I do not always realise You are. Please help me to remain honest with You and remember that You will always answer my 'whys' in the best way, Your way. Amen.

Like gold

'But if I go to the east, he is not there; if I go to the west, I do not find him. When he is at work in the north, I do not see him; when he turns to the south, I catch no glimpse of him. But he knows the way that I take; when he has tested me, I shall come forth as gold.' **JOB 23:8–10**

Job was still mouthing his complaints to God and the list was growing longer each day. He felt so frustrated. God had allowed him to get in this mess without showing him a way out. He wanted a showdown. He wanted answers to his questions. And he wanted them now!

But what had Job learnt while he waited for God to act? First, Job had examined his life in micro detail to see if he was in the wrong. And after much heart searching he knew there wasn't any unconfessed sin separating him from God. Suffering sometimes motivates us to flush out the household germs and get our lives back in line with God.

Second, although he couldn't get answers from God, he knew God was around. **He realised God was testing his faith.** And if he kept trusting God he would come through his experience as 'gold' (v10).

To get pure gold you have to melt it under intense heat. All the impurities rise to the surface as dross and are skimmed away.

So instead of cursing God, Job decided to follow Him more closely. And keep talking to Him even though it was so frustrating not to get immediate answers.

 God sometimes allows the heat to be turned up to deal with the dross in our lives. Are you experiencing some painful trials at the moment? By examining our lives and getting close to God we can emerge as better and stronger people for the experience.

Question!

'Then the LORD spoke to Job out of the storm. He said: "Who is this that obscures my plans with words without knowledge? Brace yourself like a man; I will question you, and you shall answer me. Where were you when I laid the earth's foundation? Tell me, if you understand … Who shut up the sea behind doors … Have you ever given orders to the morning … Have the gates of death been shown to you? … Tell me, if you know all this."' **JOB 38:1-4,8,12,17-18**

Do you treat God like the ultimate encyclopedia? Forever asking Him to turn up answers to all of your problems? Often God wants us to do the thinking and the working out. And He does that by raising issues and questions for us to think through.

Suddenly Job was forced to stop thinking that the world revolved around him and his problems. God arrived as quizmaster, with creation as the specialist subject.

Job was speechless. He hadn't a clue how God made the universe, or the sea, or the clouds. Or how to control sunrise or sunset. Neither did he know much about life and death issues when it came down to it.

Job suddenly felt very small. He'd been mouthing off without knowing much about God and His power. **He suddenly realised how limited his thinking was.** He began to appreciate the greatness of God and His plans. Nothing happens by accident. God knows what's going on and is in total control.

Job started looking at the world from where God was standing and his problems seemed a lot, lot smaller.

God sometimes answers our questions with questions. And if we can come through a difficult time having worked out the good it has brought us, we will be better for it. Suffering raises more questions than answers, but those questions can help us work things through with our God. Is God raising any issues with you at the moment? What have you got to say on the matter?

Forgive

'After Job had prayed for his friends, the LORD restored his fortunes and gave him twice as much as he had before. All his brothers and sisters and everyone who had known him before came and ate with him in his house. They comforted and consoled him … The LORD blessed the latter part of Job's life more than the former part.' **JOB 42:10–12**

Job was sorry for the way he'd directed his anger and frustration at God. But he'd learnt a lot about his weaknesses and God's strengths.

God took Job's friends to task for the misleading advice they had given him. They'd gossiped that Job must have been bad to get such harsh treatment from God, and tried to send him off on a guilt trip.

Job was asked to pray for those who had added to his hurt while he was down. And when he did so, **God moved in to mend his broken heart** and life. Job didn't have to queue at the job centre. God found him a new business, which became more successful than the last. His wife stopped complaining and his brothers started being supportive. He also had seven sons and three daughters. As for his health problems – he lived to be 140!

Job stopped being a patient and became known for his patience. He had learnt to hang on in there and trust God.

 Engage

Bitter experiences can leave bitter roots. That's why it's important to pray for those who have added to our difficulties and forgive them. The deeper our wounds the harder it is to forgive those who have inflicted them, but we must. It can't have been easy for Job to pray for those who had falsely accused him, but he did. And it opened the way for the healing process to begin.

Pray

Lord Jesus, I choose to forgive [insert name] who has hurt me, even though I might not feel like it. Help me to continue to pray for them, as You want me to. Amen.

That's better!

'When the LORD restored the fortunes of Zion, we were like those who dreamed. Our mouths were filled with laughter, our tongues with songs of joy. Then it was said among the nations, "The LORD has done great things for them." The LORD has done great things for us, and we are filled with joy. Restore our fortunes, LORD, like streams in the Negev. Those who sow with tears will reap with songs of joy. Those who go out weeping, carrying seed to sow, will return with songs of joy, carrying sheaves with them.'

PSALM 126:1–6

God put the Israelites through the sieve while they were in Babylon. The impurities were sifted out and dealt with. God then gave them their return tickets.

God's 'vine' did grow again. **Those who returned to rebuild Jerusalem and the Temple were stronger in their faith.** This psalm celebrates God's kindness to them and the benefits of God's 'pruning'.

Travellers walking up the long, winding road to Jerusalem would sing this 'psalm of ascent' to remind them of the great way God had turned them around. Just look at the quality of fruit growing on the vine too:

- Laughter had replaced tears.
- Songs of joy replaced laments.
- They were filled with happiness not misery.
- Others noticed the difference the Lord had made to their lives.
- They were keen to talk about the great things God had done for them.

God wants His Spirit to flow through life, reviving the parts that need to be reached. The Negev desert lies to the south of Jerusalem, a vast expanse of wilderness – empty, lonely and unproductive. And that's how Christians can feel at times. But God restores us as 'streams in the Negev' (v4) – refreshing, reviving and life-giving!

Always there

'Remember your Creator in the days of your youth, before the days of trouble come and the years approach when you will say, "I find no pleasure in them" – before the sun and the light and the moon and the stars grow dark, and the clouds return after the rain … Remember him' **ECCLESIASTES 12:1–2,6**

Getting older was a sobering experience for Solomon. And he wanted to do what older people like to do – give young people the benefit of his advice.

Now this wasn't the kind of advice you hear today, like:
- You only live once.
- Make the most of it while you're young.
- Enjoy it while you can.
- If it feels good, do it.

Solomon's advice was to put God first in your life while you are young: 'Remember your Creator in the days of your youth.'

Don't put God on hold, planning to take Him more seriously when you get older. God is not just for middle age, He's for now. You'll make most of the major decisions in your life over the next few years. Bring God in on them; don't leave Him off the agenda.

Solomon had another reason for advising you to put God first in your life while you're young. You'll have someone to turn to in all of life's troubles. And troubles there could well be.

Look at Ecclesiastes 12:5. Even grasshoppers can find that life's a drag. God never makes out we'll go through the whole of life with a spring in our step but He does promise to be with us wherever we are. And help to carry our burdens.

 **Engage** **When the heat is turned up to unbearable, don't look to get out, look to get close to God.**

Pray

Father, when life gets hard, help me to get closer to You. Thank You that You'll never let me down. Amen.

Heart of Jesus

'As Jesus walked beside the Sea of Galilee, he saw Simon and his brother Andrew casting a net into the lake, for they were fishermen. "Come, follow me," Jesus said, "and I will send you out to fish for people." At once they left their nets and followed him. When he had gone a little farther, he saw James son of Zebedee and his brother John in a boat, preparing their nets. Without delay he called them, and they left their father Zebedee in the boat with the hired men and followed him.'

MARK 1:16–20

Jesus' heart was for God and for people – you and me. When He left Nazareth to begin His teaching ministry, He made His base at Capernaum on the shores of Galilee. It was a town brimming with tension and, like a lot of places we may know, was home to a diverse collection of people, all with different beliefs and ideas.

As we explore this exciting time in the Bible, we're going to get more out of it if we remember that the words Jesus said were also meant for you and me! So as we look at these passages, really think over how Jesus' actions and words could affect your life, your decisions and your relationship with God.

In today's verses we see a very important moment: Jesus calling His first disciples. And how quickly did these men respond to His call? 'At once'! That's right, **no hesitation, no questions, no doubts.** Jesus extends the same invitation to us. And we have this choice: follow Him or carry on the way we are.

What do you think of Jesus' way compared to our own ways? How would you describe it to someone else? Perhaps it could be summed up with its destination: an eternity with God, in paradise!

Pray

Dear Lord Jesus, as I learn more about You and the time You spent on earth, I pray that You would speak to me and show me what these words mean for my life today. Amen.

With whose authority?

'They went to Capernaum, and when the Sabbath came, Jesus went into the synagogue and began to teach. The people were amazed at his teaching, because he taught them as one who had authority, not as the teachers of the law. Just then a man in their synagogue who was possessed by an impure spirit cried out, "What do you want with us, Jesus of Nazareth? …"

"Be quiet!" said Jesus sternly. "Come out of him!" The impure spirit shook the man violently and came out of him with a shriek. The people were all so amazed that they asked each other, "What is this? A new teaching – and with authority! He even gives orders to impure spirits and they obey him." News about him spread quickly over the whole region of Galilee.'

MARK 1:21–28

Jesus was a big hit in the pews. He really knew what He was talking about. As God's Son He had a pretty big advantage when it came to speaking about God. But there was trouble in the back row. One of the locals, who had probably been dabbling with the occult in the Decapolis cities or getting into new age teaching with the health gurus at the Roman baths, started shouting abuse. Or so it appeared. In reality it was the evil spirit in control of the man that was making the noise. The evil spirit was petrified! It recognised Jesus – not a part-time carpenter but 'the Holy One of God' (v24). It knew its time was up.

The Speaker confronted the shrieker and commanded the evil spirit to leave. It was out of the man and out of the town in a flash. The pews were filled with gasps. Where did the new Teacher get His authority? **Evil spirits were powerless against Him.** Little did the congregation appreciate it at the time, but they had seen God's awesome power, which changes people's lives, at work.

Do you realise that God wants to use you to show His awesome power to the people you meet and know? Yes, He cares deeply about them, even if they're really hostile towards Him. Do you know people who are hardened against God and abusive in the way they talk about Him? Pray for them. God has the power to melt their hearts of stone and fill them with His peace.

Problem!

'Jesus left the synagogue and went to the home of Simon. Now Simon's mother-in-law was suffering from a high fever, and they asked Jesus to help her. So he bent over her and rebuked the fever, and it left her. She got up at once and began to wait on them.' **LUKE 4:38–39**

Peter and his three fishing mates had first met Jesus when they were with John the Baptist. John advised them to stop following him and start following Jesus instead. Jesus helped the four fishermen to the biggest catch of fish of their lives. It was impressive, but the incident of the possessed man in the synagogue really got them thinking. Jesus had the power to dismiss evil spirits! They had seen it with their own eyes. So when Jesus came back for lunch, they didn't leave Peter's mother-in-law downstairs while they picnicked on the roof – they asked Jesus to help.

The four fishermen knew Jesus had the power to heal her. And that's what Jesus did. One minute she was flat out on her back with a fever, the next she was up and about preparing lunch! Instead of keeping their problem to themselves, the fishermen **gave the problem to Jesus.**

Peter, Andrew, James and John learnt a great lesson that day – one that was to help them for the rest of their lives. We'd do well to remember it, too!

Engage

Don't ignore problems or difficulties. Ask Jesus to help. It makes such a difference! Are there people around you facing difficulties? Why not ask Jesus to help them? Are you struggling along as best you can in a difficult situation? Ask Jesus to help. He can get you up and ready to serve Him in no time at all.

Pray

Lord Jesus, I invite You into my difficult situations or into those of others around me. Be the Healer we need. Amen.

Doctor, doctor

'At sunset, the people brought to Jesus all who had various kinds of illness, and laying his hands on each one, he healed them. Moreover, demons came out of many people, shouting, "You are the Son of God!" But he rebuked them and would not allow them to speak, because they knew he was the Messiah. At daybreak, Jesus went out to a solitary place. The people were looking for him and when they came to where he was, they tried to keep him from leaving them. But he said, "I must proclaim the good news of the kingdom of God to the other towns also, because that is why I was sent." And he kept on preaching in the synagogues of Judea.' **LUKE 4:40–44**

The nearby hot springs attracted visitors looking for cures for aches, pains, ailments and illness from all over the Roman Empire. There were six large baths and a seventh reserved for special use. At night when the area was clear, lepers and diseased outcasts were allowed to use this seventh pool. Around the pools bogus doctors sold potions and cures. They prayed to the Greek goddess Hygeia who was thought to have healing powers – but with no result. Capernaum was surrounded by seriously ill people desperately seeking help.

News of the synagogue incident and the healing of Peter's mother-in-law led to an invasion of Capernaum. But would Jesus bother to see them? To their deep relief, Jesus turned Peter's house into a surgery and gave each one an appointment. **No one was turned away.** Those who were sick were healed. Those possessed with evil spirits were freed.

There wasn't a name on the surgery door but the evil spirits who were booted out knew the name of this Doctor – 'You are the Son of God!' The truth was out!

 Engage

Many people in your neighbourhood are looking for answers. Most are still searching for real meaning to life. Some have tried every gimmick and trend going without success. So what should you do? Do what the friends of these sick people did and introduce them to Jesus. He will not disappoint them or turn them away.

Pray

Lord Jesus, please help the people I know who are sick and hurting. Amen.

Meet in the middle

'A few days later, when Jesus again entered Capernaum, the people heard that he had come home. They gathered in such large numbers that there was no room left … Some men came, bringing to him a paralysed man, carried by four of them. Since they could not get him to Jesus because of the crowd, they made an opening in the roof above Jesus by digging through it and then lowered the mat the man was lying on. When Jesus saw their faith, he said to the paralysed man, "Son, your sins are forgiven … I tell you, get up, take your mat and go home." He got up, took his mat and walked out in full view of them all. This amazed everyone and they praised God, saying, "We have never seen anything like this!"'

MARK 2:1–5,11–12

Four men were so convinced Jesus could heal their paralysed friend that **they didn't give up on what seemed impossible.** The house with Jesus inside was full and surrounded. No way in. Do you ever feel distant from God, like there's an obstacle in the way? Well, look at what these guys did – they persevered. They clawed a hole in Peter's baked mud roof and lowered their friend to Jesus. And Jesus stopped His preaching to do the very best thing He could – forgive his sins.

It was a pretty impressive miracle to heal the paralysed man so he could get up, roll up his mat and walk out of the building, but that was a minor benefit compared to forgiving the man's sins and reserving him a place in heaven.

The proud Pharisees present were secretly accusing Jesus of blasphemy for claiming He had the right to forgive sins. But when they saw the paralysed man jumping up and down on his bed they burst out in praise to God. The logic was this: if Jesus had God's power to get a paralysed man on his feet, He must also have the power to forgive sin. And if He could forgive sin, He must be God.

Engage

As followers of Jesus, we can go through times when we can't feel or hear God, or we think that God isn't listening to us. There's an amazing promise in the Bible, which is, 'Come near to God and he will come near to you' (James 4:8). So press on in prayer and worship, push past the things holding you back; God promises to meet you halfway.

Change

'Once again Jesus went out beside the lake. A large crowd came to him, and he began to teach them. As he walked along, he saw Levi son of Alphaeus sitting at the tax collector's booth. "Follow me," Jesus told him, and Levi got up and followed him.' **MARK 2:13–14**

On the down side, Matthew (also known as Levi) was disloyal and a cheat. Tax collectors were money mad, charging more than they needed and pocketing the difference. And as Capernaum was on the junction of two major trading routes, Matthew was raking it in.

On the up side, you had to be fairly intelligent to be a tax collector. It required accountancy skills beyond adding up on your fingers and toes, plus the ability to write.

Jesus knew He could deal with the down side of Matthew and use the up side. Years later, Matthew was to use his scribing skills to write his Gospel about Jesus. The hand that once penned dodgy accounts was transformed to write a true account. And millions of people throughout the world have learnt about Jesus because of Matthew.

At the time it didn't seem very bright to invite one of the most unpopular men in town to become a disciple. It was bound to cause trouble with the other disciples. It could even lead to Jesus being labelled as a friend of tax collectors. But **Jesus is in the business of changing people.** He never gave up on Matthew and He won't give up on you either.

 So who is the person you least like in your neighbourhood? ... In your school? ... In your church? It may be very hard but the first step in overcoming your dislike for someone is to pray for them. God sees their hearts and their potential and He can help you see their 'up side' too.

Pray

Lord God, please help me see other people as You see them. Amen.

The wrong crowd

'Then Levi held a great banquet for Jesus at his house, and a large crowd of tax collectors and others were eating with them. But the Pharisees and the teachers of the law who belonged to their sect complained to his disciples, "Why do you eat and drink with tax collectors and sinners?" Jesus answered them, "It is not the healthy who need a doctor, but those who are ill. I have not come to call the righteous, but sinners to repentance."'

LUKE 5:29–32

The local Pharisees, mostly businessmen, tradesmen and merchants from up-town Capernaum, had already had their noses put out by Jesus. He was a much better teacher than they were and was very popular in the area. So when they saw Him eating a blow-out meal with Matthew, his tax collecting friends and other dubious characters, they started pointing the finger. The Pharisees refused to eat or mix with those known to break their laws or work for the Romans – it just wasn't done. Accepting an invite for a meal was a sign that you were good friends with your host. So when Jesus turned up at Matthew's house it caused quite a stir. What was He up to?

Jesus had come to get close to people. He hates bad behaviour, but He loves the people. And He knew He couldn't help them change their ways by refusing to speak to them. As Jesus put it – **if you are a doctor you don't keep away from the sick** but visit them. And if you're the Saviour of the world you reach out to those who need forgiveness, which is exactly what Jesus does. He is always prepared to spend time with us.

Engage

God wants us to mix with those who aren't Christians so we can introduce them to Him. The danger, of course, is that we try to earn the acceptance of those who aren't Christians by becoming more like them in their attitudes and actions. We need to accept others without accepting the wrong things they do. Ask Jesus to help you get this right.

acceptance

Reach out

'Another time Jesus went into the synagogue, and a man with a shrivelled hand was there. Some of them were looking for a reason to accuse Jesus, so they watched him closely to see if he would heal him on the Sabbath. Jesus said to the man with the shrivelled hand, "Stand up in front of everyone." Then Jesus asked them, "Which is lawful on the Sabbath: to do good or to do evil, to save life or to kill?" But they remained silent. He looked around at them in anger and, deeply distressed at their stubborn hearts, said to the man, "Stretch out your hand." He stretched it out, and his hand was completely restored. Then the Pharisees went out and began to plot with the Herodians how they might kill Jesus.' **MARK 3:1–6**

The Pharisees had made up over 600 rules and regulations for keeping the Sabbath as a rest day. On Friday at 6pm, a trumpet sounded three times from the roof of the synagogue to announce the start of the Sabbath. At 6pm on Saturday, the trumpet sounded to announce the Sabbath was over. The atmosphere in the synagogue was hostile.

In the back rows was a man with a paralysed hand. Would Jesus heal him on the Sabbath? This was something the Pharisees considered totally out of order. Jesus told the man to stand up. As He looked around at the critical faces watching Him, He was deeply upset by their attitude. **They didn't care about this poor man at all.** All they cared about was themselves and their laws. What could be wrong with doing good on the Sabbath? Jesus ignored them and asked the disabled man to reach out towards Him. As he reached out to Jesus he was healed. Were the Pharisees praising God? No – they sulked off to plot with the supporters of the Roman governor to assassinate Jesus (so much for their rules about keeping away from foreigners).

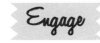 **Some people put pressure on us to not go to Jesus for help. They don't even need to say anything – a hostile look can be enough. Don't ever let anyone stop you from getting closer to the Person who cares deeply about you.**

Jesus, thank You for always being within reaching distance. Help me to remember that today. Amen.

Such faith

'The centurion heard of Jesus and sent some elders of the Jews to him, asking him to come and heal his servant. When they came to Jesus, they pleaded earnestly with him ... So Jesus went with them. He was not far from the house when the centurion sent friends to say to him: "Lord ... say the word, and my servant will be healed. For I myself am a man under authority, with soldiers under me. I tell this one, 'Go', and he goes; and that one, 'Come', and he comes. I say to my servant, 'Do this', and he does it." When Jesus heard this, he was amazed at him, and turning to the crowd following him, he said, "I tell you, I have not found such great faith even in Israel."'

LUKE 7:3–4,6–9

It was the job of the Roman centurion to keep law and order in the area. He had built the synagogue to keep on friendly terms with the Jews. No doubt he had had Jesus closely watched. News of His miracles was drawing large crowds to the town. One of his tax collectors, Matthew, had deserted to become a disciple of Jesus. Yet, reports that the centurion gathered didn't point to Jesus being a troublemaker but a person with the power of God.

So when his servant became terminally ill, he bypassed all the Roman doctors and gods and went downtown to find Jesus. This was amazing! Romans had a terrible track record for despising and mistreating the Jews. Why didn't the centurion order Jesus to come to him? And

why did he speak to Jesus with such respect?

The centurion could expect his orders to be carried out as he had the authority of the Roman emperor. He had worked out, however, that if Jesus was God, all He had to do was give the command to heal his servant. His faith in Jesus was far in advance of any Jew.

We have a powerful God. The difficulty, sometimes, is realising it. We constantly underestimate God's power to change lives and situations. Step one is going to Jesus to tell Him 'we're not worthy'. Step two is trusting that you can leave a problem with God because He has the power to sort it out. Why not take two steps in the right direction now?

Help

'When this man heard that Jesus had arrived in Galilee from Judea, he went to him and begged him to come and heal his son, who was close to death … The royal official said, "Sir, come down before my child dies."

"Go," Jesus replied, "your son will live." The man took Jesus at his word and departed. While he was still on the way, his servants met him with the news that his boy was living. When he enquired as to the time when his son got better, they said to him, "Yesterday, at one in the afternoon, the fever left him." Then the father realised that this was the exact time at which Jesus had said to him, "Your son will live." So he and his whole household believed.'

JOHN 4:47,49–53

Jesus helped the poor and down-and-outs in Capernaum. He helped those with bad reputations for crime and immoral behaviour. He even helped the local Roman centurion. But would He help this official working for Herod? Remember that some of Herod's officials were plotting to assassinate Jesus.

The official reached Jesus at 1pm, probably disturbing His siesta. He grovelled in the dust, pleading with Jesus to return to Capernaum with blue lights flashing. Jesus didn't move. Did this official really believe He would heal his son?

The answer was 'Yes'! Had the Roman centurion told him about the authority and power of Jesus? Most likely he had! Jesus didn't have to be on the scene to release God's power into a situation. The official kept pleading with Jesus to act. Jesus gave the heavenly royal orders for the boy to be healed. The official did not know it at the time, but back in Capernaum his son was jumping out of bed fit and well. He set off for home trusting that Jesus would keep His word. **Jesus was his only hope.** And when he met up with his servants rushing out of Capernaum to bring him the medical update, he discovered Jesus had not let him down.

Jesus doesn't hold any grudges or prejudices against anyone. Rich, poor, respectable or wild, upper, middle or lower class, Jews or foreigners – Jesus helps anyone who needs help. Do you need help? Do you know someone else who needs help? Then turn to Jesus and do something practical.

Don't be afraid

'when [Jairus] saw Jesus, he fell at his feet. He pleaded earnestly with him, "My little daughter is dying. Please come and put your hands on her so that she will be healed and live." So Jesus went with him … Jesus told him, "Don't be afraid; just believe." … When they came to the home of the synagogue leader, Jesus saw a commotion, with people crying and wailing loudly. He went in and said to them, "Why all this commotion and wailing? The child is not dead but asleep." … he took the child's father and mother … and went in where the child was. He took her by the hand and said to her, *"Talitha koum!"* (which means "Little girl, I say to you, get up!"). Immediately the girl stood up and began to walk around'

MARK 5:22–24,36,38–42

Jairus was president of the synagogue in Capernaum. He had been responsible for the services when Jesus had delivered a man from an evil spirit and healed a man with a paralysed hand. His friends were the Pharisees, who we've seen were critical of Jesus. But when his 12-year-old daughter became seriously ill, he knew where to turn.

Jesus agreed to travel into up-town Capernaum, where the posh houses were, to visit the girl. But His progress was hindered by the huge crowd pushing through the narrow streets. Too late! Before they reached the house, news broke that the girl was dead. However, the words 'too late' don't apply to Jesus. His timing is never out. Jesus ignored the crowd's advice, 'Don't bother'. **It's impossible for Jesus to stop caring.**

How did Jairus feel? Jesus has a powerful word in his ear: 'Don't be afraid; just believe!' Then He walked by his side into the rich neighbourhood. The Pharisees never touched a dead body as it made them 'unclean', a rule that Jairus was meant to enforce. But Jesus held the dead girl's hand and told her to get up. Immediately she did just that. It was an awesome demonstration of God's power.

Engage

Jesus didn't desert Jairus. He stayed by his side during the most distressing moments of his life. And that's where you'll find Jesus when you get overwhelmed – right next to you! Why not talk with Him now? Don't be afraid; just believe.

Daughter

'a woman was there who had been subject to bleeding for twelve years … When she heard about Jesus, she came up behind him in the crowd and touched his cloak, because she thought, "If I just touch his clothes, I will be healed." Immediately her bleeding stopped and she felt in her body that she was freed from her suffering. At once Jesus realised that power had gone out from him. He turned round in the crowd and asked, "Who touched my clothes?" … Then the woman, knowing what had happened to her, came and fell at his feet and, trembling with fear, told him the whole truth. He said to her, "Daughter, your faith has healed you. Go in peace and be freed from your suffering."'

MARK 5:25,27–30,33–34

This woman was not allowed to touch anyone. Her illness, which led to severe bleeding, made her 'unclean'. While unclean she had to warn others to stay away and she was forbidden to enter the synagogue.

That's why she crept up behind Jesus to touch Him. That's why she trembled when she realised Jesus knew what she had done.

So why did the woman bother to touch the hem of Jesus' cloak? Jesus, like all Jewish men, wore a rectangular cloak placed over His head that covered His upper body. On the four corners of the garment hung tassels of blue and white linen, required by the law of Moses (Num. 15:37–40). These tassels came to symbolise a person's power and authority. By touching a tassel on the garment of Jesus, the woman believed she could experience God's power to heal her. And her faith made her well. It was also the custom that only family members could touch the tassels on a father's garment. When Jesus spoke to the woman it was not to reprimand her but to call her 'daughter'. Isn't that wonderful! Not only was she healed but **she was made 'clean' to become a member of God's family.**

Engage

There are people in your town who are desperate to meet Jesus but they just don't know how to go about it. Some may feel so 'unclean' they fear Jesus would reject them anyway. Pray for anyone you know who may feel like this. Don't pass up opportunities to spread the news that Jesus welcomes anyone who comes to Him.

Respect

'After Jesus and his disciples arrived in Capernaum, the collectors of the two-drachma temple tax came to Peter and asked, "Doesn't your teacher pay the temple tax?"

"Yes, he does," he replied. When Peter came into the house, Jesus was the first to speak. "What do you think, Simon?" he asked. "From whom do the kings of the earth collect duty and taxes – from their own children or from others?"

"From others," Peter answered.

"Then the children are exempt," Jesus said to him. "But so that we may not cause offence, go to the lake and throw out your line. Take the first fish you catch; open its mouth and you will find a four-drachma coin. Take it and give it to them for my tax and yours."' **MATTHEW 17:24–27**

Jesus had every reason to evade paying His Temple taxes. He knew the money was finding its way into the pockets of the Temple leaders – those who made His life difficult whenever He went near Jerusalem. More than that, why should He as God's Son cough up for God's house? Kings didn't expect their sons to pay taxes to them so why should He fund God's work?

There were two good reasons why Jesus paid His taxes in full. He knew God wanted Him to live as a law-abiding citizen in Capernaum. The tax system was unfair but it was His duty to obey the authorities that ruled the land.

The second reason was so that **He didn't cause offence.** No one was able to accuse Him of dishonesty or cheating, which would have discredited His teaching. The top officials in the town respected Him.

And Jesus didn't raid the disciples' funds set aside for the poor to pay His taxes. He set up a species of fish that swallows shiny objects (now known as Peter's fish) to come on line to cough up the money. Honesty does pay!

 Engage

We are to set a standard by our honesty and willingness to obey God's commands. And what about those school rules that are just waiting to be broken? Don't even think about it ... no matter how unfair or daft they may seem. Yes, honouring parents is part of the deal too.

Pray

Lord Jesus, please help me to get this area of my life right so I can earn the respect of those around me. Amen.

The offer of Jesus

'Then Jesus began to denounce the towns in which most of his miracles had been performed, because they did not repent. "Woe to you, Chorazin! Woe to you, Bethsaida! For if the miracles that were performed in you had been performed in Tyre and Sidon, they would have repented long ago in sackcloth and ashes. But I tell you, it will be more bearable for Tyre and Sidon on the day of judgment than for you. And you, Capernaum, will you be lifted to the heavens? No, you will go down to Hades. For if the miracles that were performed in you had been performed in Sodom, it would have remained to this day."'

MATTHEW 11:20–23

After all the good Jesus did for the inhabitants of Capernaum, most turned their backs on Him. When He died on the cross, although there were thousands from Capernaum visiting Jerusalem at the time, none came to His rescue.

Jesus described Capernaum as being worse than the infamous city of Sodom. Had the notoriously wicked inhabitants of Sodom seen the miracles of Jesus they would have turned to God in repentance.

But the people of Capernaum had hardened their hearts against God, and the result was that the town would face God's judgment. Years later, at a date we do not know, Capernaum was destroyed by volcanic activity. It has never been rebuilt.

Some of the locals, however, did believe. Peter, Andrew, James and John, plus Matthew among the men, and many women too. We know that a church met in Peter's house. Inscriptions on a wall that can still be seen today have the name 'Jesus' on them, referring to Him as 'the Lord, the most high God'.

When Jesus is at work in a place, **some will believe but many will reject Him.** Little do they know they are rejecting so much.

Most people have no time for Jesus. Some may be anti-Jesus and anti-Christian too. Do we give them up as a lost cause? No – not while there are opportunities to rescue people into God's family. Ask God to fill you with the Holy Spirit so you'll have the boldness to live for Jesus. Worship Jesus in your community as the most high God!

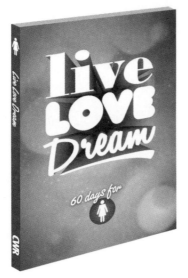

**You are wonderfully made.
A genuine original.
Totally unique.
The one and only you!**

You have the potential to live an extraordinary life and this gorgeous little book wants to celebrate just that! From self-image to sharing the gospel with friends, discover what the Bible has to say, and what God has in store for you, every day.
ISBN: 978-1-78259-100-9

Available from **www.cwr.org.uk/youth**

Also available online or from Christian bookshops

YP's daily devotional – dig deeper into God's Word

Never did reading the Bible look so good! Get eye-opening, jaw-dropping Bible readings and notes every day, plus special features and articles in every issue (covers two months).

Available as individual issues or annual subscription. For current prices and to order visit

www.cwr.org.uk/youth

Also available online or from Christian bookshops

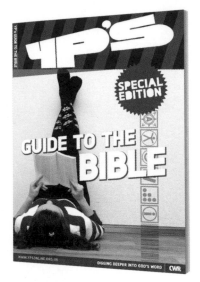

Get to know and understand the Bible

Written to help you know and understand the Bible
better, this exciting full-colour guide includes key
events, maps, timelines, major characters, explanations
of biblical terms and so much more!
ISBN: 978-1-85345-352-6

For current prices and to order visit
www.cwr.org.uk/youth

Also available online or from Christian bookshops